Simple Solutions

Barking

Plus Training Tips

By Kim Campbell Thornton
Illustrations by Buck Jones

BOWTIE™
P R E S S

IRVINE, CALIFORNIA

Ruth Strother, Project Manager
Nick Clemente, Special Consultant
Amy Fox, Editor
Michael Vincent Capozzi, Designer

The dogs in this book are referred to as *he* and *she* in alternating chapters.

Library of Congress Cataloging-in-Publication Data

Thornton, Kim Campbell.
  Barking / by Kim Campbell Thornton ; illustrations by Buck Jones.
     p. cm. -- (Simple solutions)
  ISBN 1-889540-81-1 (pbk. : alk. paper)
  1. Dogs--Barking. 2. Dogs--Behavior. 3. Dogs--Training. I. Dog fancy (San Juan Capistrano, Calif.) II. Title. III. Series.
  SF433 .T52 2001
  636.7'0887--dc21
                                    2001004823

BOWTIE™
P R E S S

A DIVISION OF FANCY PUBLICATIONS
3 Burroughs
Irvine, California 92618
949-855-8822

Printed and Bound in Singapore
10 9 8 7 6 5 4 3 2 1

Contents

Why Do Dogs Bark?

Dogs bark for any number of reasons. They bark when someone approaches their territory, in response to other dogs, and sometimes in response to noises, such as sirens. They bark at squirrels and other potential prey. Some breeds are born to bark; it's in their nature. Often dogs bark in excitement, such as when they know they are going for a walk, taking a car ride, or getting their dinner. Occasionally, barking is stress related, a sign of separation anxiety. Sometimes dogs bark just because they're bored.

Researchers have found that dogs almost always have a

reason for barking. Barking is a complex means of close-range communication, and dogs make a number of basic vocal sounds. Their barks often express various emotions, such as loneliness, fear, distress, and pleasure. For instance, a stressed dog—say, one who's left home alone—has a high-pitched, atonal, repetitive bark. Noisy barks are usually defensive in nature, while harmonic barks occur in play and other social contexts.

Just as people in different parts of the world have different accents and languages, different dog breeds have

subtle variations in their types of barks. These variations

are believed to correspond to dialects. And even the

sounds people use to describe dog barks vary from country to country, from *woof-woof* in English to *jau-jau* in Spanish to *wung-wung* in Chinese. Is this because our dogs are speaking different languages, or are we simply not paying careful attention to what they're saying?

Dog-to-English Dictionary

If you pay close attention to your dog, you can learn to decipher her different barks. To get you started, here are some "translations" from canine ethologists (people who study dog behavior):

- A rapid string of three or four barks with pauses

between each series means, "Let's get together. There's something we need to check out."

- Rapid barking at a midrange pitch is an alarm meant to alert other dogs or people. It usually occurs when a stranger enters the territory.

- Continuous barking at a slower pace and lower pitch than the alarm bark indicates an immediate threat.

- Bark and pause, bark and pause, bark and pause for a long period of time indicates a dog is lonely.

- One or two short, sharp barks is a typical canine greeting.

- A single loud bark means, "Knock it off!" Dogs often do this when they're awakened from a nice nap or their tail is tugged by a playful puppy.

- Puppies use insistent barks to get attention.

- Some dogs learn to call their owners when it's dinnertime or when they'd like to go outside. They usually do this with a single, purposeful bark.

- A dog whose bark rises in level of intensity is excited or having a good time.

Who Barks and Why?

Some dog breeds have been bred to bark. Perhaps the most well-known barking breeds are the terriers. These specialized hunting dogs, whose original purpose was to follow their prey into underground dens or burrows, needed to have some way of letting their people know where they were in case they got stuck underground. Barking was much more effective than, say, collars with bells, which had the drawback of getting stuck on roots underground and were sometimes difficult to hear. People who kept terriers for hunting began selecting dogs who barked loudly when they were excited. They bred them with other dogs who had this trait, and before long, all terriers were barkers. Other breeds that tend to bark a lot include beagles, keeshonden, cocker spaniels, and herding breeds, such as Shetland sheepdogs.

The basenji, on the other hand, is known as the barkless breed. The basenji does make noise, although the sound is usually described as a soft howling or yodeling. It's not that basenjis can't bark; they just seldom do so unless they're terribly excited. Why don't basenjis bark? We don't know, but it may be that silence was safer for dogs in the African wilds, where the basenji first originated. It may also simply be a genetic trait for this particular breed.

The tendency to bark is very likely the result of a dominant gene. When dogs who don't bark much are bred with dogs who bark a lot, puppies are much more likely to bark than not bark. Researchers have not found whether female dogs bark more than male dogs or vice versa. Purebreds and mutts are equally likely to bark excessively.

Dogs can also learn to bark from each other. A dog who has learned to bark appropriately is invaluable in teaching

a new puppy what kind of bark is necessary for asking to

be let outside or how long to bark when people come to

the door. However, a nuisance barker can teach bad habits to a new dog. And just as humans sometimes pick up the accent of the place where they live, dogs can learn to copy the intonations of other dogs' barks.

When Barking Becomes a Problem

The most important thing to know about barking is that it is a normal dog behavior. At appropriate times and levels, barking is even considered to be a useful behavior. Many people get dogs because they want them to bark when someone is either coming to the door or prowling around at night. But when barking becomes excessive, the noise can be a real headache for owners and their long-suffering neighbors. According to the Cornell Animal

Behavior Clinic, up to one-third of behavioral complaints

involve nuisance, inappropriate, or excessive barking.

Before things get out of hand, take steps to teach your

dog when it's okay to bark and when she should stop or remain quiet. If you want her to bark when people approach the house, enlist your kids, spouse, or a neighbor to help with the training. Ask the helper to come to the door and knock or ring the doorbell. If your dog doesn't bark at the noise, encourage her by excitedly asking, "Who's there? Is someone at the door?" Praise your dog when she barks at the sound.

Once your dog is barking to alert you, the next step is to teach her when to stop. After she has given a couple of barks, hold up your hand and say a code word or command, such as *enough* or *quiet*. Give the command in a firm, quiet tone of voice. If you yell, your dog will simply think you're barking back at her, and she'll just bark more.

If your dog stops barking, praise her—"good quiet!"—and pop a treat into her mouth. Be sure you give the praise and treat only when the dog is quiet.

Often, showing the dog a treat may be distraction enough to stop the barking. Say, "quiet," and give her the treat after several seconds of silence. As your dog starts to learn what the word *quiet* means, extend the amount of time between saying the command and giving the reward.

Some trainers recommend wrapping your hand around your barking dog's muzzle, or snout, and saying, "quiet" or "no bark." That works sometimes, but you have to be careful when trying that technique. If your dog is barking frenziedly, she may accidentally bite you when you try to wrap your hand around her muzzle.

A safer way to get this effect is to keep a halter collar on your dog while you're at home. This type of collar has a loop that wraps around your dog's muzzle. When your dog barks more than once or twice, give a quick pull on the lead to tighten the loop around the muzzle. As soon as the dog is quiet, say, "good no bark" or "good quiet," and reward her with a treat.

Another way to stop the barking is to call your dog to

you or give her a down command. Calling your dog to you usually interrupts barking. And a dog hardly ever barks when lying down. Choose a command such as *come* or *down* and use the same one every time. Offer praise for silence and then reward your dog with a treat.

Be sure you don't unintentionally reward your dog for barking by hugging her or saying soothingly, "It's okay, Sweetie." When you do that, the dog thinks she must have been right to bark. This simply encourages her to bark more the next time a similar situation occurs.

Solving a Barking Problem

When you're trying to retrain a dog who barks excessively, the first step is to figure out why he is barking. Dogs are social animals, and most often, excessive barking occurs when they're left outdoors all the time with little human contact and nothing to occupy them. If your dog is bored or anxious, punishment is not an appropriate response to the barking. The solution is to understand why he's bored or anxious and deal with the problem. You might find that your dog is seeking attention or even trying to defend his territory. Videotaping the dog while

you're gone can help you figure out at what point barking

starts, as well as what sets it off.

Bored Barney

The most important way you can solve barking problems resulting from boredom is to let your dog inside the house, especially when you're at home. Teach your dog to act appropriately in the house so he can live with you instead of being tied out in the backyard. That's no life for a dog.

There are times in every dog's life, though, when he needs to stay alone. Help make these times bearable by providing interactive toys such as Kongs and Buster Cubes, which can be filled with food. Hide the toys around the house so your dog has to work to find them. One innovative trainer recommends packing a "sack lunch" for your dog. Fill a paper bag with treats and toys, tape it up, then leave it for your dog to get into on his own. He'll spend his time trying to get at the treats instead of barking his head off. To prevent boredom, rotate the toys and vary the types of treats you use. Occasionally, substitute cream cheese for peanut butter or liver biscuits for cheese-flavored mini bones.

Exercise is an important part of relieving boredom. Walk the dog or play fetch before you leave. If possible, have a

neighbor or pet-sitter come in during the day to help
break up the monotony with a walk or a little playtime.

Fretful Fido

Anxiety is a common cause of problem barking. Anxious dogs, like bored dogs, are usually lonely. It's important to help these dogs learn to relax through behavior modification. Start by getting your dog used to being left alone for short periods. Put your dog in his crate with a treat. Don't make a fuss about leaving; instead, be matter-of-fact about it. Stay away for only a minute or two so your dog doesn't have time to become anxious and start barking. Gradually extend the amount of time you leave the dog alone. Make sure he has a toy to play with, and consider

leaving the radio or television on so he can hear human voices.

A crate serves as a valuable tool for helping anxious

dogs. Crated dogs are cozy and comfortable in their special place, freed of the responsibilities of being on their own. Dogs who are rewarded with a treat for entering their crate often are delighted when they hear the word *crate* and race to see who can get there first. Outdoor dogs may find a similar sense of security if they have access to a doghouse or are confined to a dog run.

Another way to help reduce anxiety is to vary your routine before leaving. Dogs quickly pick up on visual cues, such as putting on a coat or pulling keys out of a purse. Change your routine by doing things in a different order or

going through the motions but then staying home. Eventually, your dog will learn to ignore these cues and relax.

Behavior modification takes time, so be patient. In severe barking cases, a veterinary behaviorist may have to prescribe medication to smooth out the process. Medication isn't a quick fix, though, and won't solve the problem without behavior modification.

Talkative Tank

Some dogs just won't shut up. They love hearing the sound of their own voice, and once they get started, they don't stop. If your dog simply won't quit barking when people come to the door—or in other situations when you're present—and you haven't had any success with training, use of a crate, behavior modification, and plenty of family interaction and exercise, you may need to turn up the intensity.

If your dog keeps barking, give him a loud verbal signal—"Aaaaack!" or "No!"—followed by a correction, such as a squirt of water from a spray bottle or tossing a throw pillow or a shake can (made by placing a few pennies in a clean, empty soda can and taping over the top) in his direction. Don't hit your dog with the objects. The goal of these actions is to make your dog realize that prolonged barking has unpleasant consequences. You need to teach

your dog that you are in control of the situation. Once he has alerted you, he needs to be quiet and let you take over.

Spot in the Spotlight

Dogs often bark too much when they want attention. The best way to deal with an attention-seeker is to ignore the barking. This is especially important with a puppy, whom you need to teach early on that you won't respond until he *stops* barking.

Dogs may also bark because they want something. They want to eat, they want to go out, or they want to play. It's important to make sure that your dog doesn't train you to respond to his barked demands. Always wait until he has been quiet for at least thirty seconds before you give him

what he wants, such as giving him a meal, letting him out

of his crate or into the yard, or tossing his ball. If you give in even once, your dog will have learned that he can manipulate you by barking, and it will take a long time to retrain him.

If you can see a pattern to the barking, take steps to break it. For instance, if your dog barks at the same time every morning because he wants out of his crate, wake up a few minutes early (before he starts barking), take him outside to do his business, then put him back in his crate, and go back to bed. Ignore further barking (wear earplugs if you have to). Your dog will learn that barking will not get him any kind of attention whatsoever.

It's very important to ignore attention-seeking barking. Walk away from the dog if you have to, but don't yell at him or thump the top of his crate. That simply gives the dog the response he wants, even though it's a negative response. When your dog finally does stop, be sure to give him an extra special reward: a favorite game or a tasty treat.

Just an Excitable Dog

Excitable dogs who bark nonstop during play simply need a chance to calm down. Bring down the intensity of the game or take a break from play until the dog is under

control. If a squirrel or a bird triggers the behavior, take the dog inside. When he's quiet, start the game again. Your behavior will teach your dog that too much barking puts an end to the good times.

Territorial Aggression

Dogs are extremely observant, and they learn quickly that barking at strangers seems to drive them away. So a dog who's allowed to stand at the door or run along the fence and bark at people has his behavior reinforced frequently when people walk by the house or when mail carriers stuff the mailbox and then depart. *I bark; they leave,* the dog thinks. If this type of barking is permitted without correction, it can lead to territorial aggression.

You can prevent problems by teaching your dog to look to you for guidance when strangers approach.

Correct him when he barks at people who are merely walking by the house, and have your mail carriers and delivery people work with you to teach your dog not to bark at them. Provide the "stranger" with treats and ask him or her to approach you and the dog. As long as the dog remains quiet, the person can toss treats to the dog, while otherwise ignoring him. Once the dog has relaxed and is no longer showing interest in barking at the person, you and the dog can walk away. This can also work if your dog barks at approaching people while you're out for a

walk. Set up a similar situation with a friend or neighbor.

Go slowly with this type of training. You want your dog to learn to trust your judgment and to feel comfortable in the presence of accepted strangers. It may take days or weeks of work before you achieve this.

If You Want Your Dog to Act As a Watchdog

Teaching your dog what *not* to bark at is the first step in developing watchdog abilities. If your dog always barks at squirrels or birds or the mail carrier, she'll never develop any discrimination, and you'll never know when to pay attention to her barking. Keep in mind as well that proper alarm barking may not develop until the dog is mature, at eighteen months to two years of age.

A good watchdog barks only when someone is attempting to enter the house or in the presence of dangerous situations, such as fires. Pay attention to what your dog barks at so you can correct promiscuous barking and praise watchdog barking. Set up situations to help teach your dog when barking is appropriate. For instance, ask a friend or neighbor to approach the house stealthily and try to enter the backdoor. Encourage your dog to bark when she hears this type of noise and praise her when she complies.

Be Patient

Just as when you're teaching any other behavior, training a dog to be quiet requires a lot of practice. Set up situations that give you the opportunity to show your dog what you want from him. Keep training sessions short—no more than five or ten minutes at a time. And no matter what techniques you use, be sure the entire family understands them and does them the same way (for example, use the same commands and praise, and be sure that everyone praises the same behaviors consistently). Consistency is one of the keys to teaching dogs success-

fully. It takes a while to teach a dog to be quiet on command, so don't give up. You didn't learn algebra in a day but in a semester or two; your dog requires plenty of learning time as well.

Bark-Control Devices

When a dog's barking is out of control and no training methods have worked to stop the barking, a bark-control collar, sometimes called an anti-bark collar, may help. This type of collar uses electronic shock, a spray of citronella scent, or sound to get the dog's attention and let her know that her behavior is unacceptable.

The correction stops when the barking does. This type of training device works best when used in combination with other behavior modification tools, such as rewarding the dog when she's being quiet and familiarizing her with the types of sounds and circumstances that cause barking, such as ringing doorbells or telephones. Do not consider a bark-control collar to be a quick fix. It's important to figure out why your dog is barking and to work on eliminating the cause or changing the dog's response to the cause. For instance, if the neighborhood kids are teasing your dog, ask them to stop or train the dog to behave differently if it continues.

How well a bark-control collar works depends in large part on the dog's personality as well as on the owner's

training skills. Bad timing or incorrect use of the collar can make the situation worse. This is especially true of electronic, or shock, collars. Dogs who are extremely timid, sensitive, or noise-shy may react negatively to the unexpected sound, feel, or scent of a bark-control collar.

Most respected dog trainers recommend against using electronic-shock training devices, which deliver an irritating shock of adjustable intensity when a vibration sensor in the collar detects barking. The potential is high for misuse and abuse of these devices. Before buying an electronic collar, consider trying the device on yourself before you use it on your dog. You may change your mind about using one.

The best choice is a collar that gives a correction using sound or a spray of citronella mist. Citronella is a fragrant grass whose oil is often used in insect repellent. Its scent is irritating but harmless. This type of collar works by releasing a spray of citronella scent whenever a microphone in the collar detects the sound of barking. In a study done at Cornell University's College of Veterinary Medicine, citronella collars were more effective than shock collars in reducing or stopping nuisance barking.

Spray collars are less aversive than shock collars and are a good first step when other methods fail to remedy nuisance barking. Don't just put the collar on your dog and leave, though. It's better to be there the first time your dog experiences the spray. Some dogs may be frightened and start to bark repeatedly, quickly using up the spray. Over time, some dogs may even learn not to bark when the collar is on but will then start barking again once the collar is off.

Sound-correction collars send out a high-decibel noise when the dog barks, serving as both an interruption and a

correction. A microphone on the collar should ensure

that the dog is corrected for only her own barking, not

that of any other dog, and the collar should be program-mable to a particular dog's level of barking. Some collars allow the owner to choose the number of barks permitted before the sound correction is set off.

No matter which collar you choose, it's best to seek advice from a qualified animal behaviorist, dog trainer, or veterinary behaviorist to find out if the product is appropriate and how to use it. This is especially true if you're a first-time user or an inexperienced dog owner. Choose a trainer who considers all other options first and who has a humane sensibility. Begin at the lowest level, and increase the collar's intensity only if necessary. Oftentimes, it only takes a couple of corrections at the lowest level to solve the problem.

Before you buy any product of this type, make sure it has safety features that prevent the collar from being misused. Such features include adjustable levels of correction and automatic shutoff so the dog isn't continually corrected. If you decide to use a shock collar, the packaging should indicate that all parts of the device are UL-certified, meaning they have passed electrical safety tests.

Ask about the availability of technical assistance either

by phone from the manufacturer's customer service department or from a local sales representative. For any type of bark-control collar, the product should have complete and easy-to-understand instructions that focus on how to change rather than control the dog's behavior. And remember that the use of such a device can cause anxious dogs to become even more nervous, making the problem worse. Some bark-control collars serve as valuable tools if they're used correctly, but they won't put an end to nuisance barking without behavior modification or eliminating the causes of boredom and anxiety.

Puppy Preschool

If your dog is a puppy, now is the time to start him off on the right paw by keeping him from developing bad habits in puppyhood. The little yapper might be cute at three months, but his noisemaking won't be cute at six months. To keep problem barking at bay, introduce your puppy to different people and expose him regularly to all kinds of sounds: vacuum cleaners, doorbells, traffic, and so on. As your dog grows older and gets used to encountering a variety of noises, people, and situations, he'll learn what requires a bark and when silence is golden.

Kim Campbell Thornton is an award-winning writer and editor. During her tenure as editor of *Dog Fancy*, the magazine won three Dog Writers Association of America Maxwell Awards for best all-breed magazine.

Since beginning a new career in 1996 as a freelance writer, she has written or contributed to more than a dozen books about dogs and cats. Her book *Why Do Cats Do That?* was named best behavior book in 1997 by the Cat Writers Association. The companion book *Why Do Dogs Do That?* was nominated for an award by the Dog Writers Association of America. Kim serves on the DWAA Board of Governors and on the board of the Dog Writers Educational Trust. She is also president of the Cat Writers' Association and belongs to the National Writers Union.

Buck Jones's humorous illustrations have appeared in numerous magazines (including *Dog Fancy* and *Cat Fancy*) and books. He is the illustrator for the best-selling books *Kittens! Why Do They Do What They Do?* and *Puppies! Why Do They Do What They Do?*

For more authoritative and fun facts about dogs, including health-care advice, grooming tips, training advice, and insights into the special joys and solutions for unique problems of dog ownership, check out the latest copy of *Dog Fancy* magazine or visit the Web site at www.dogfancy.com.

BowTie Press is a division of Fancy Publications, which is the world's largest publisher of pet magazines. For more books on dogs, look for *Chewing, Dogs Are Better Than Cats, Dogs Rule, The Splendid Little Book of All Things Dog, Why Do Dogs Do That?* and *Puppies! Why Do They Do What They Do?* You can find all these books and more at www.bowtiepress.com.